This Book Belongs to:

....

....

GRAFFITI ALPHABETS

COLORING BOOK

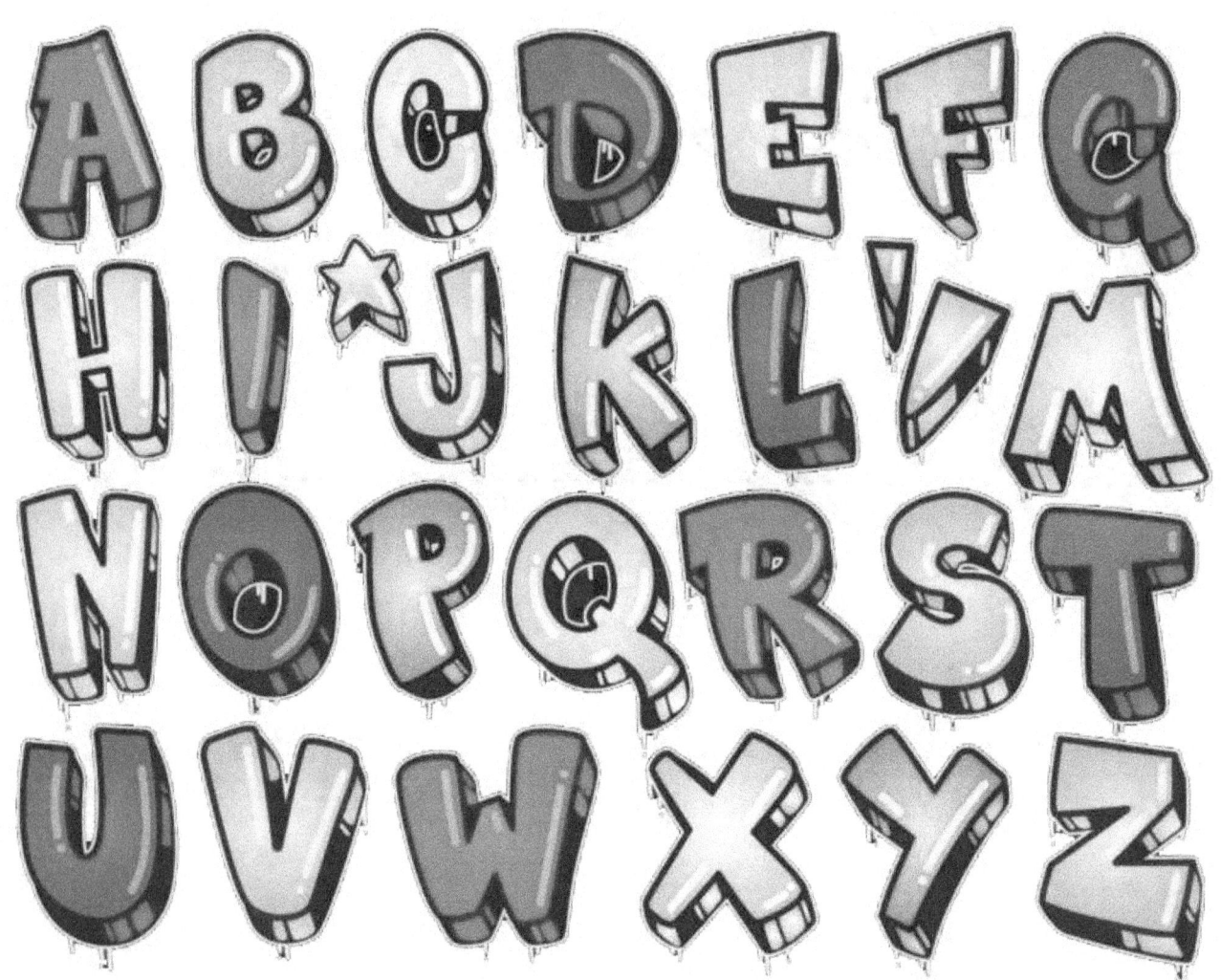

Copyright © Funny Art Press
All rights reserved. No part of this publication may be copied,
Reproduced in any format, by any means, electronic or otherwise,
Without prior consent from the copyright owner and publisher of this book

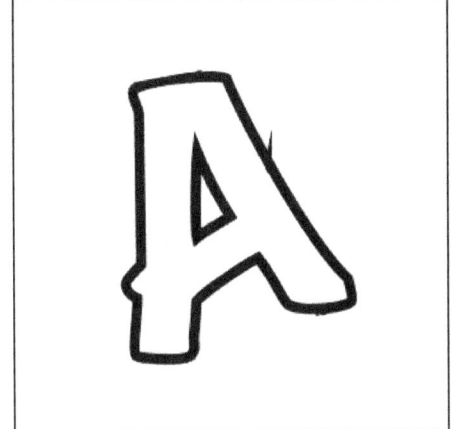
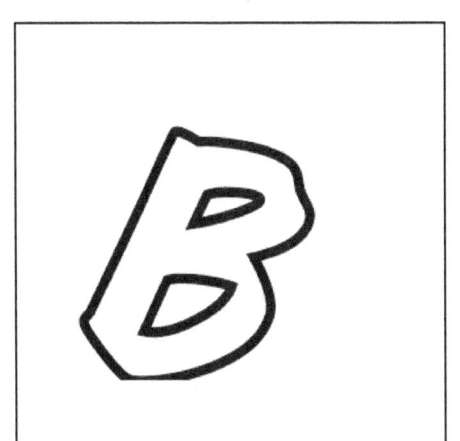
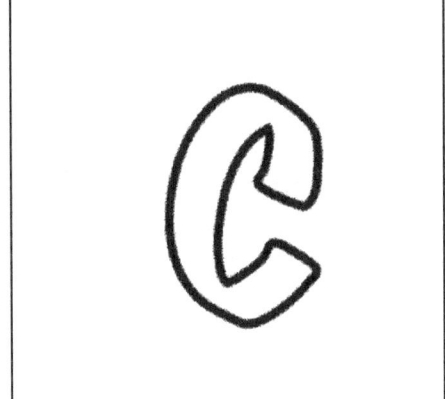
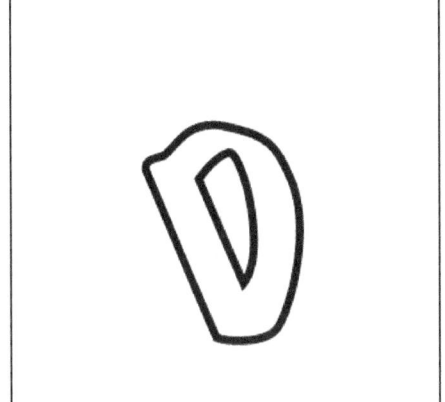

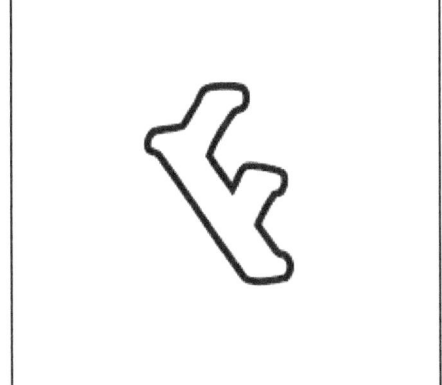

TEST COLOR PAGE
CHECK HOW YOUR COLORS SHOW OUR PAPER HERE

A

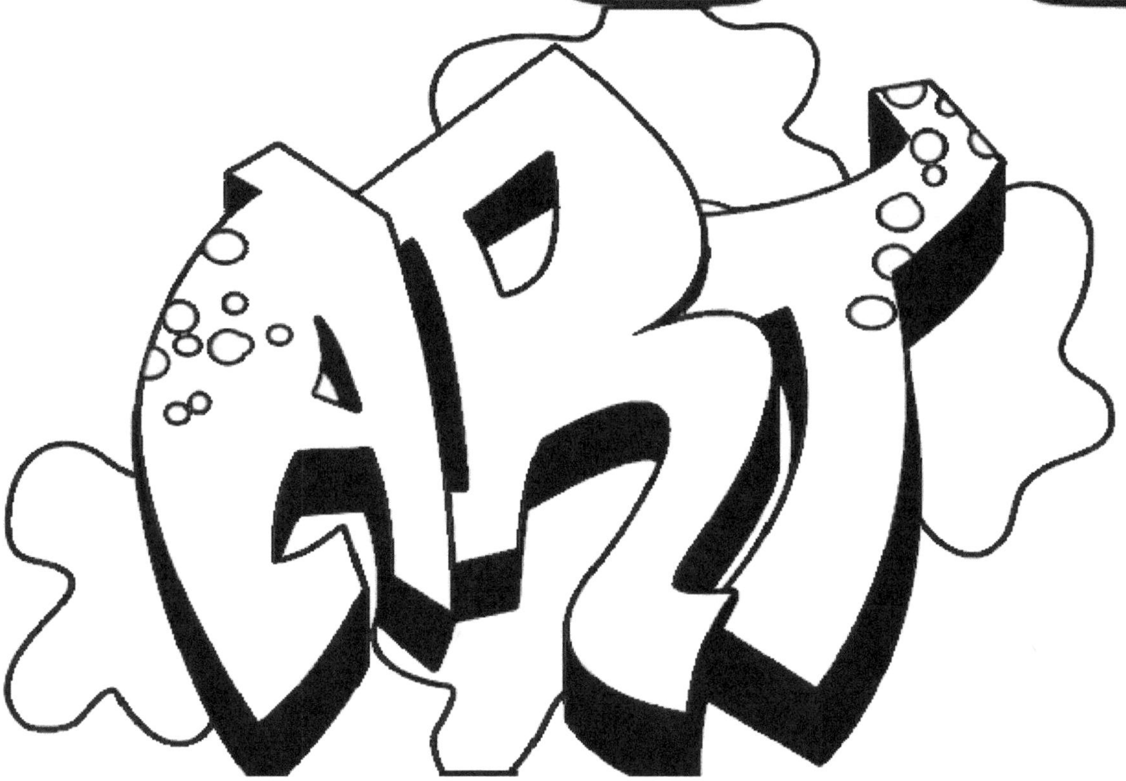

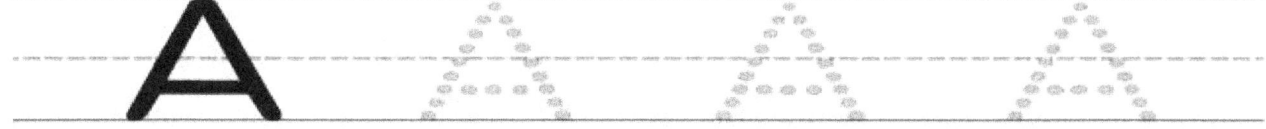

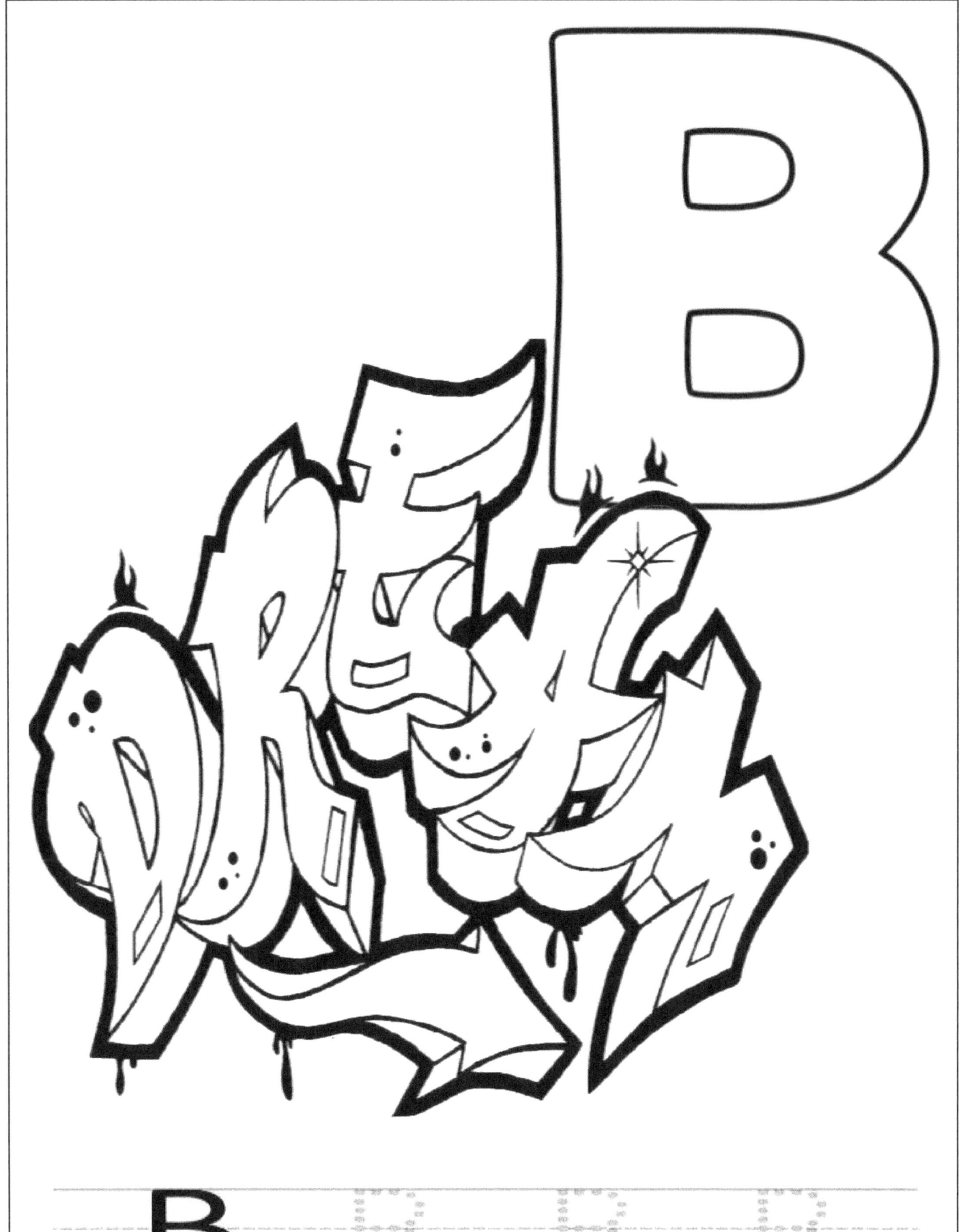

B

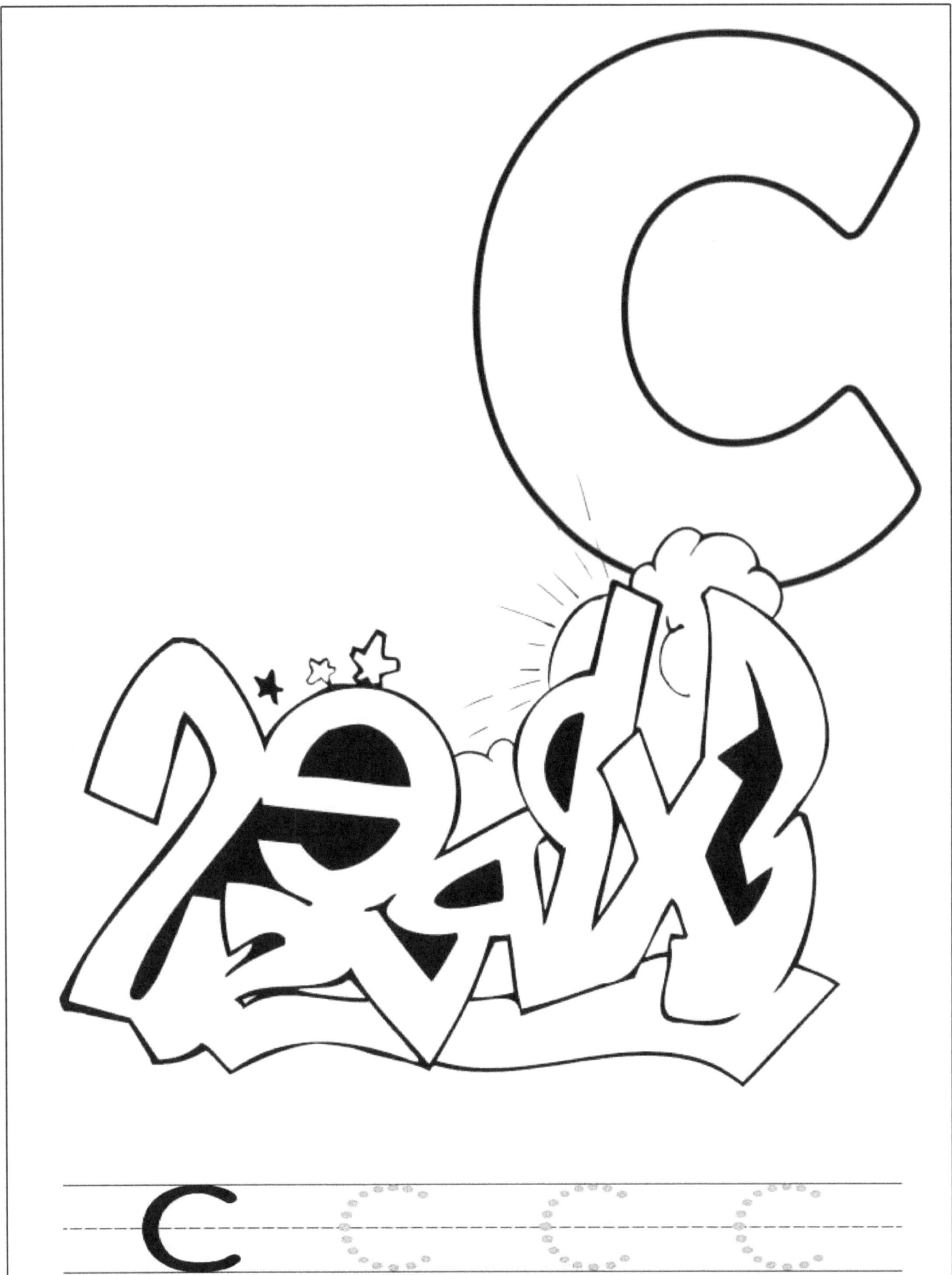

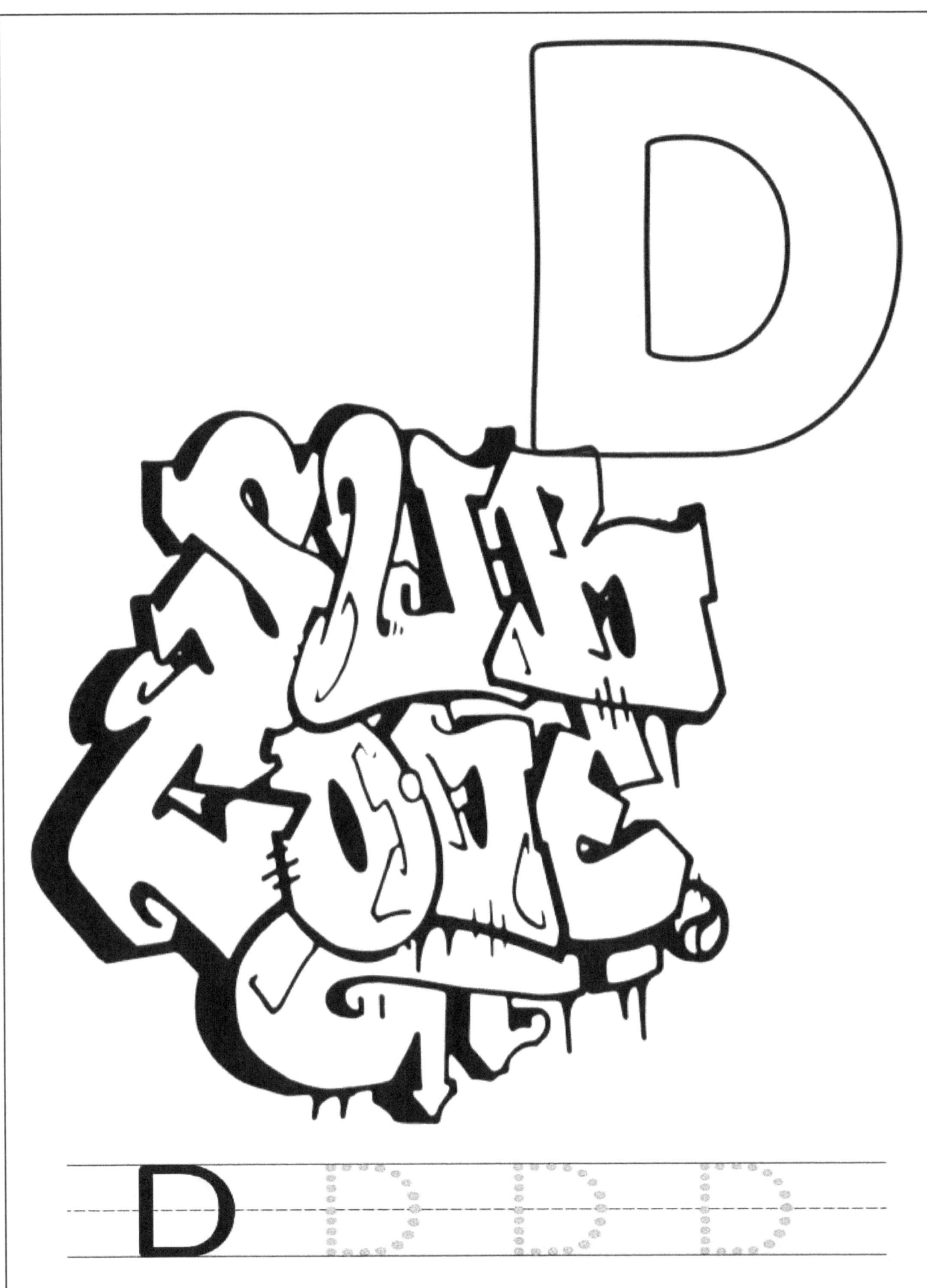

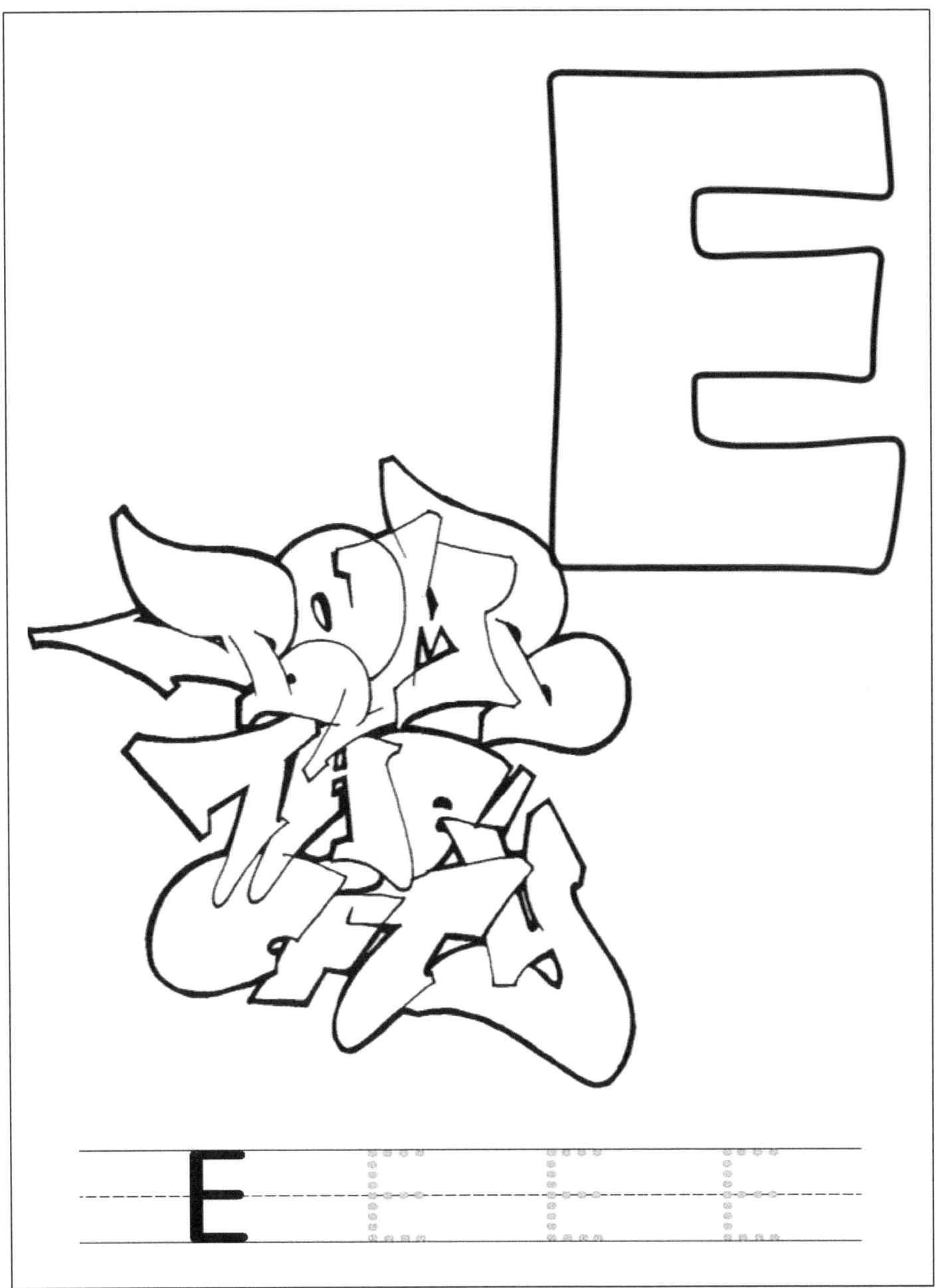

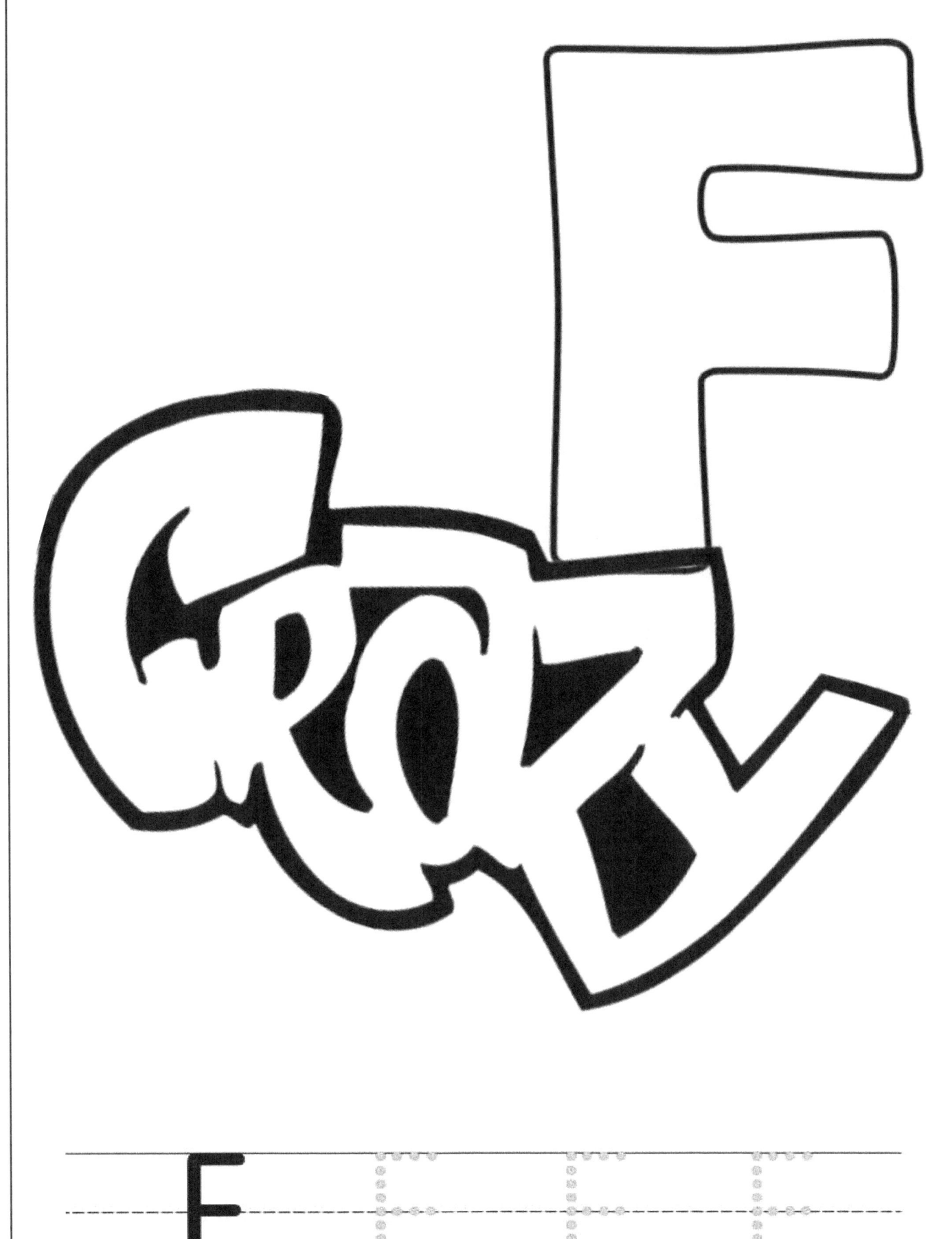

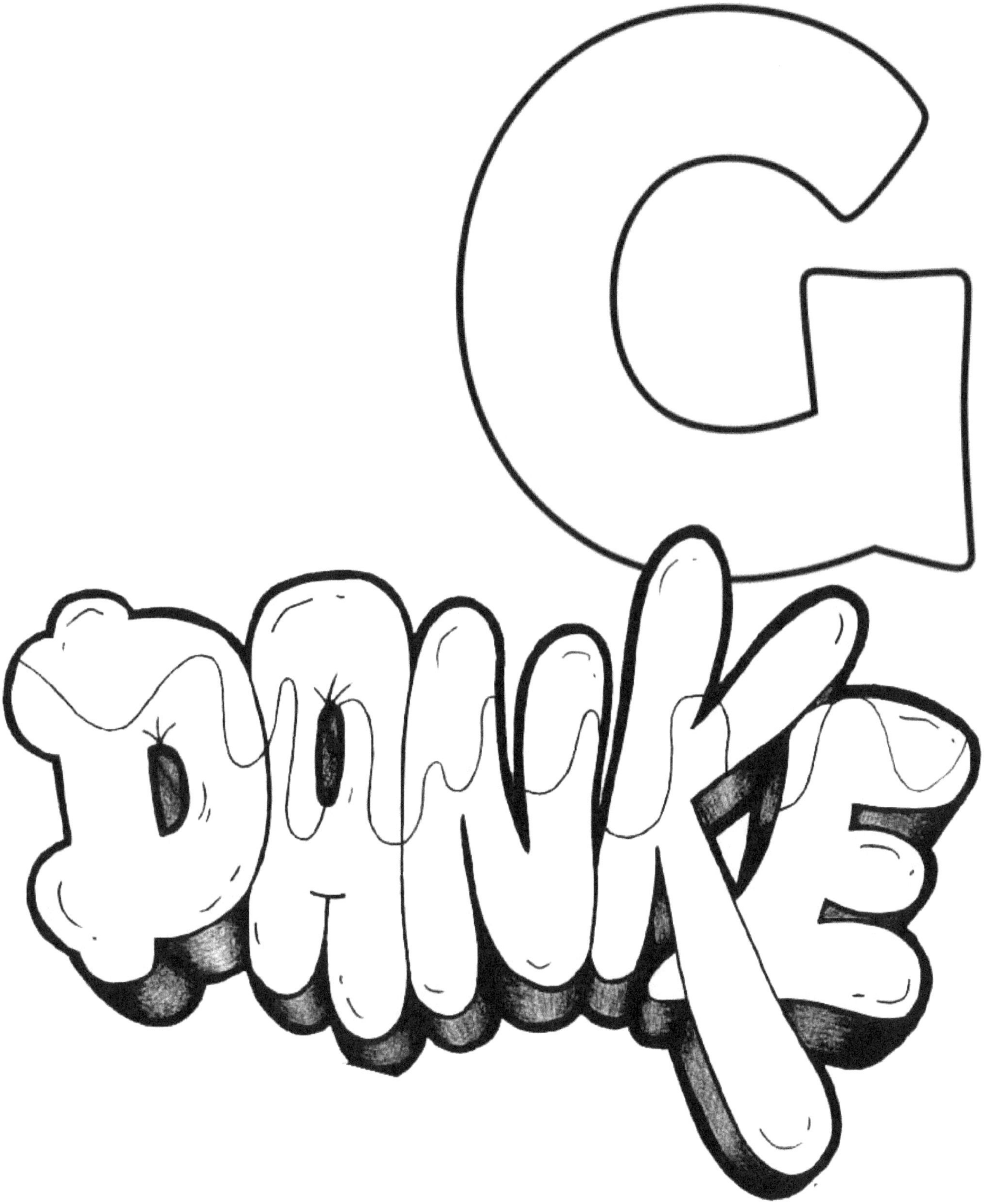

G

DANKE

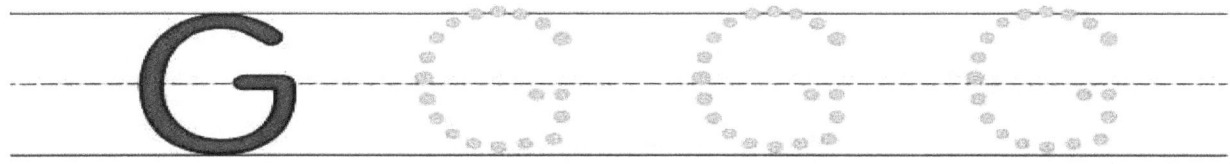

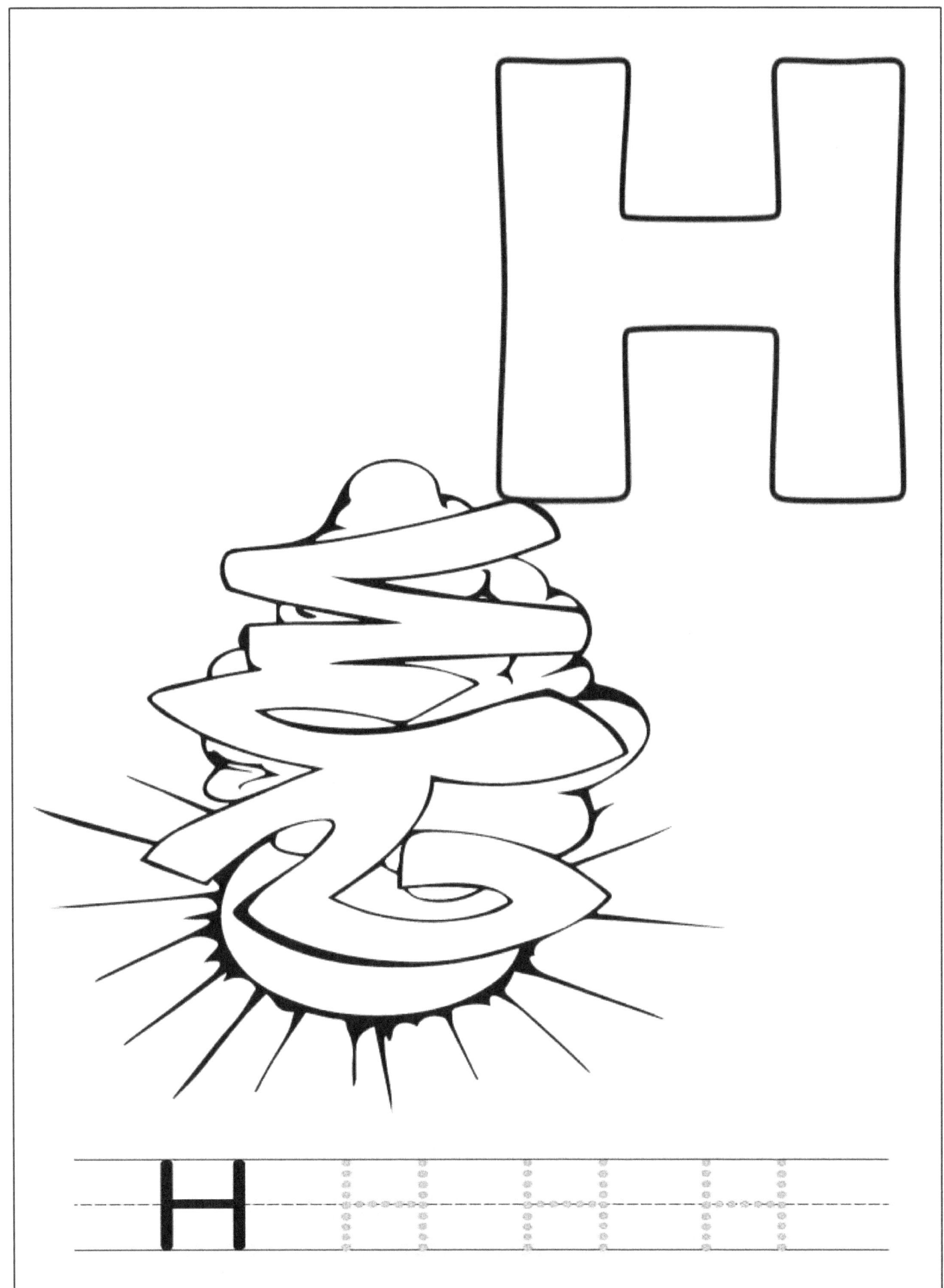

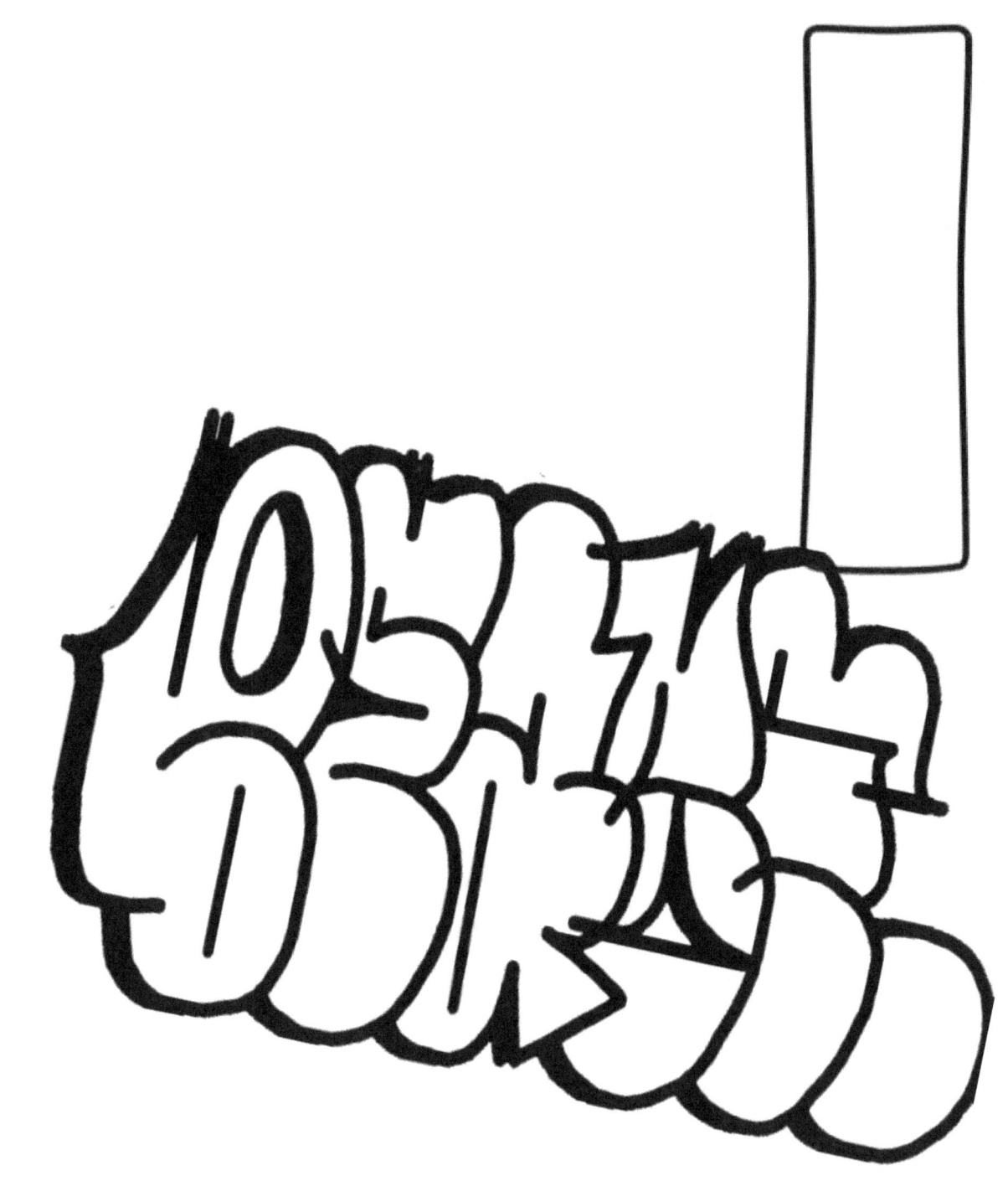

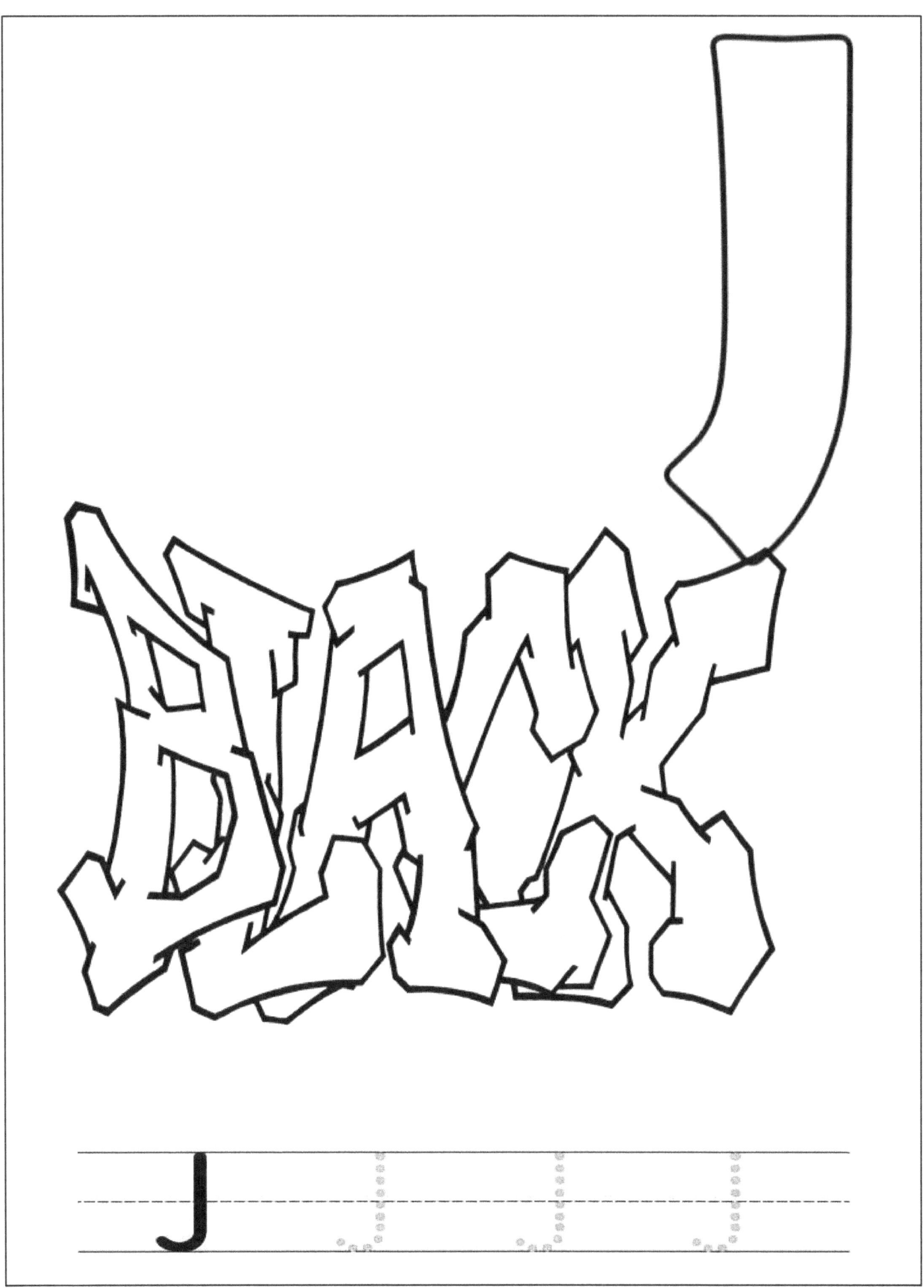

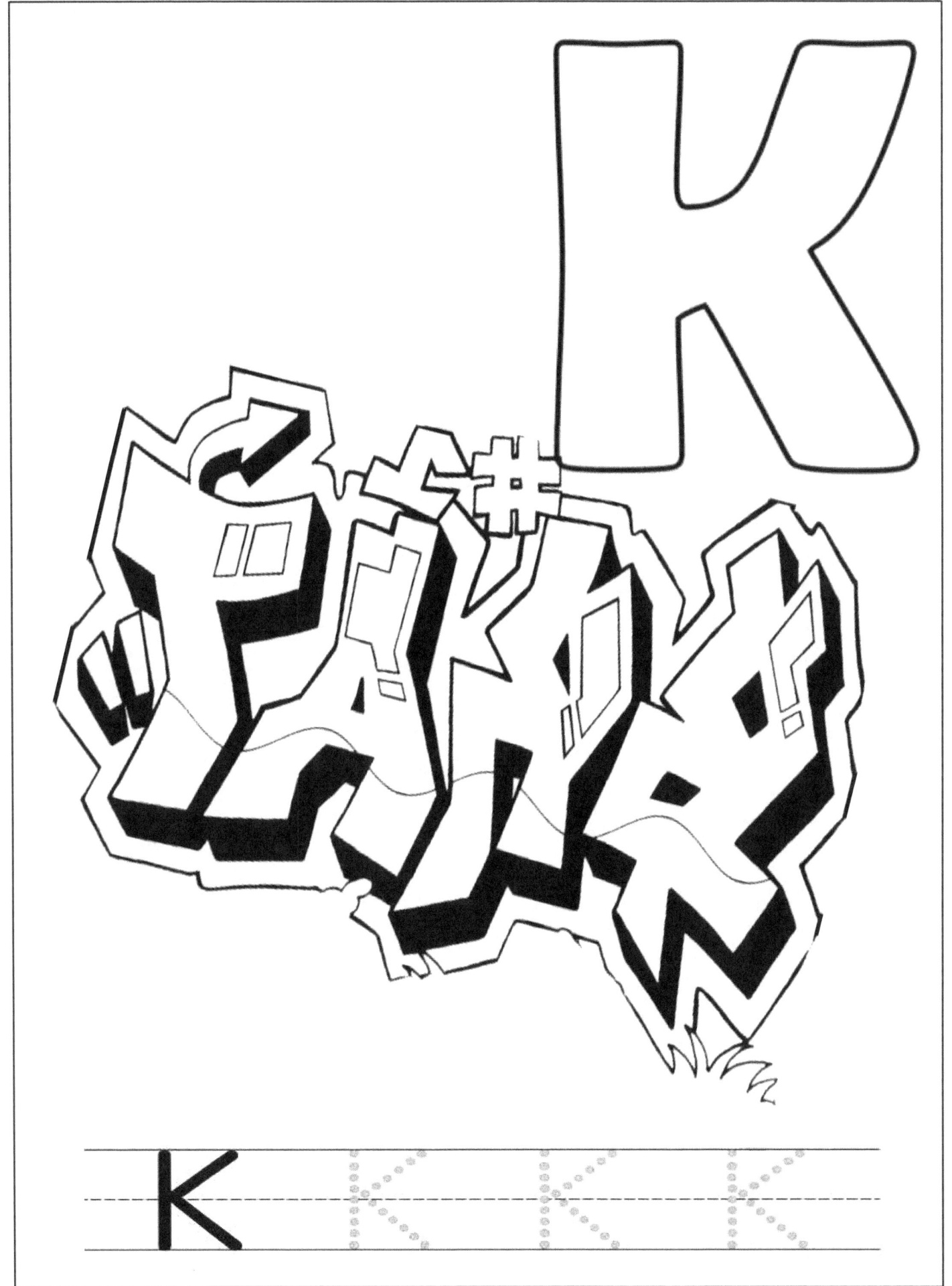

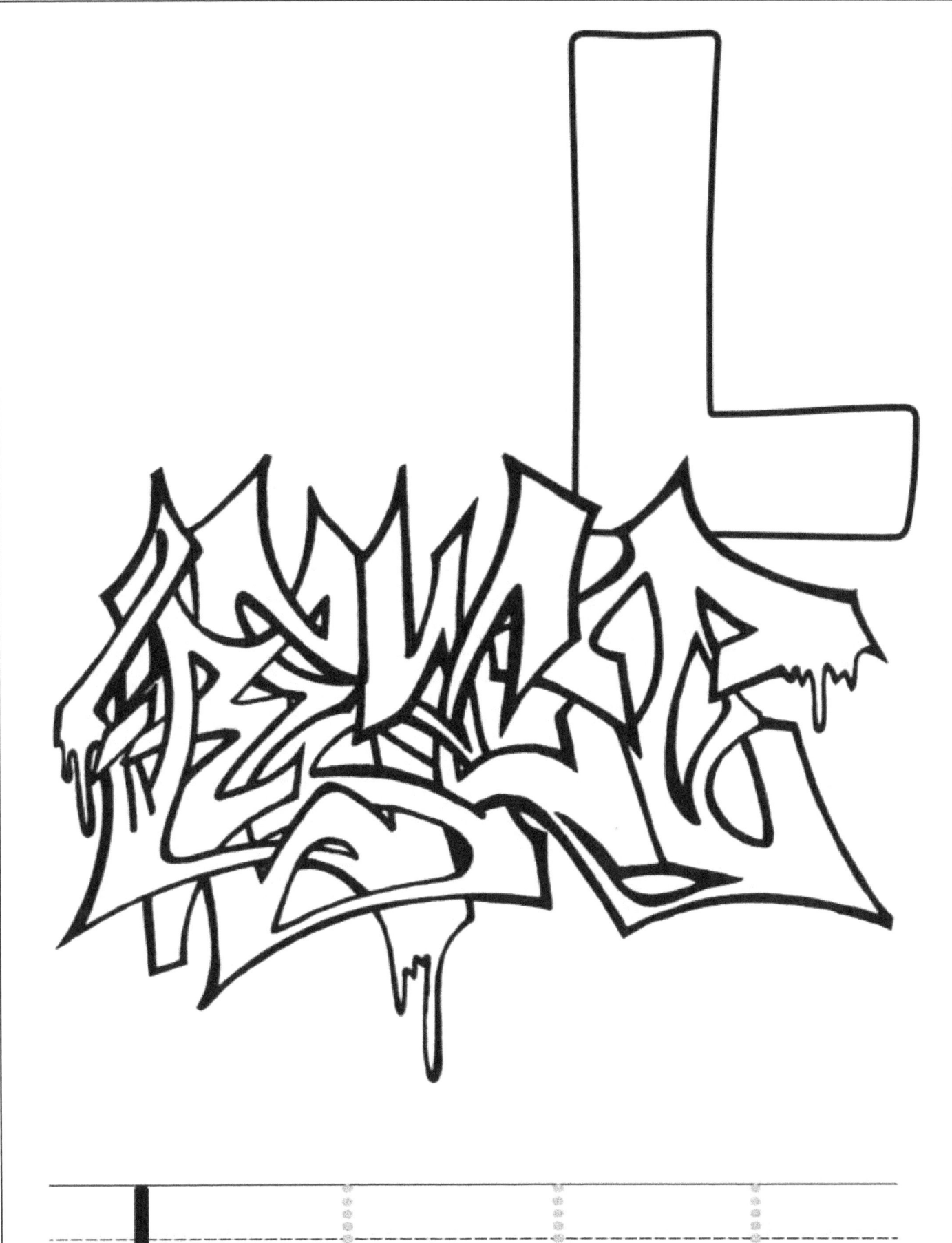

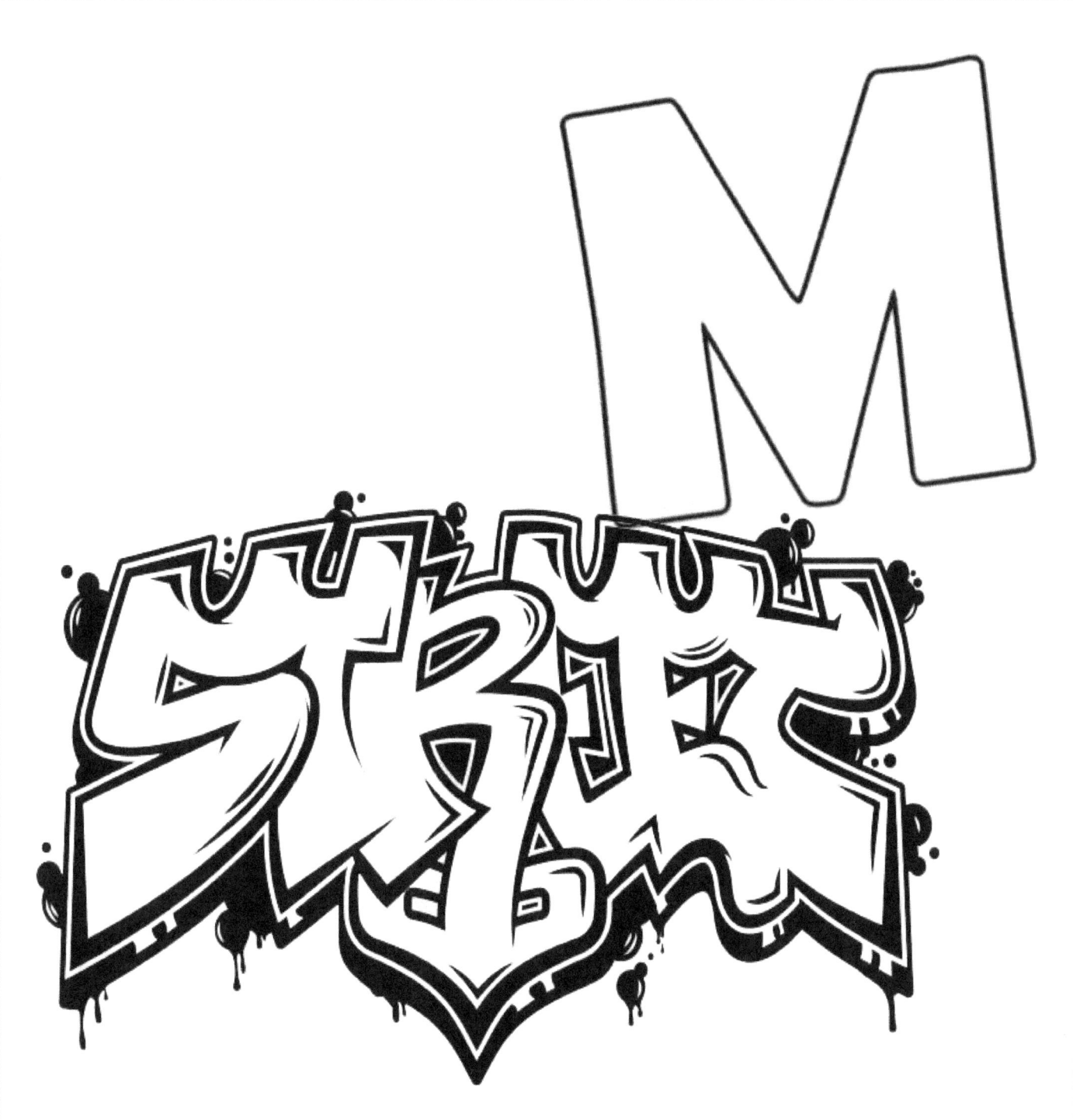

M

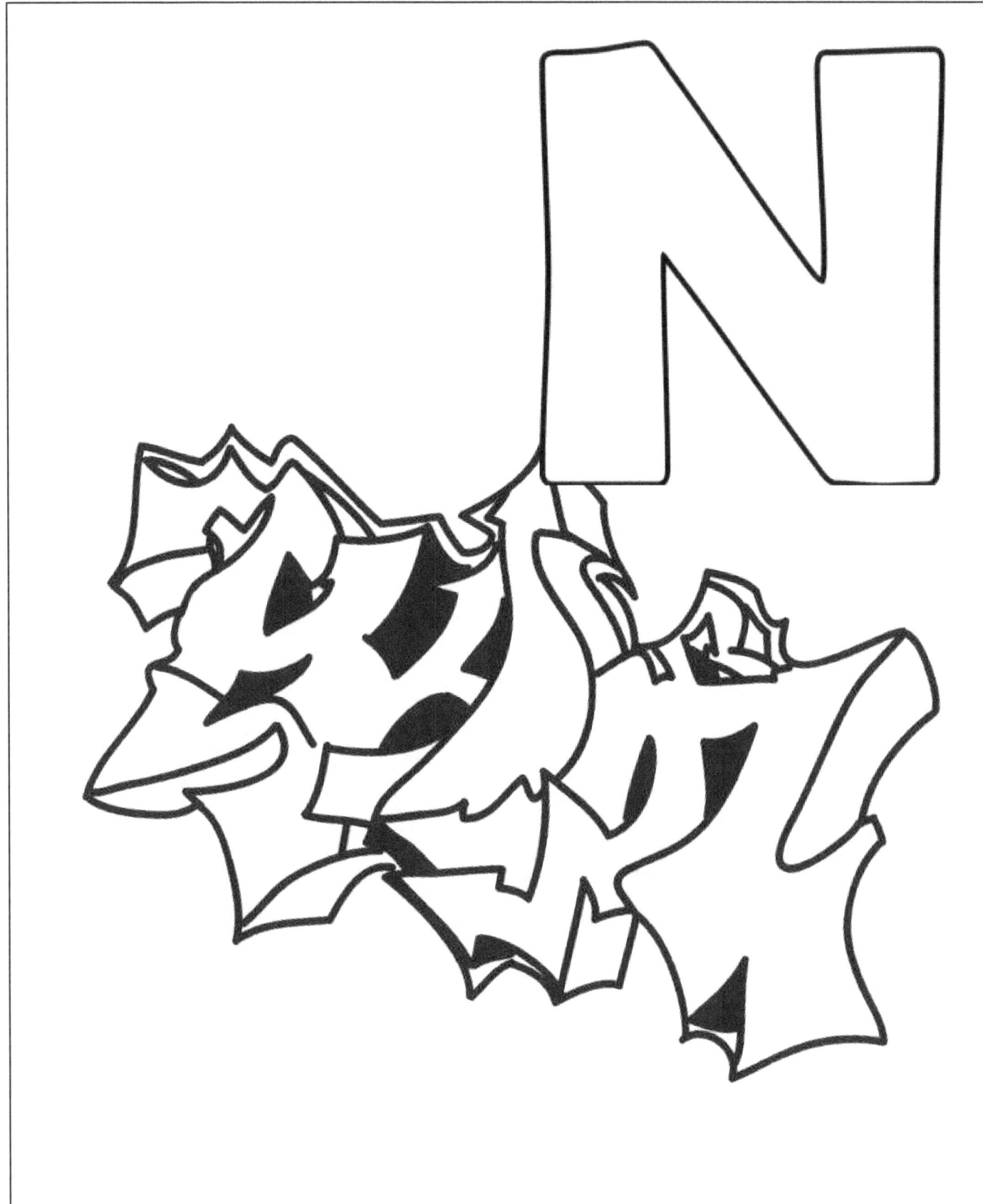

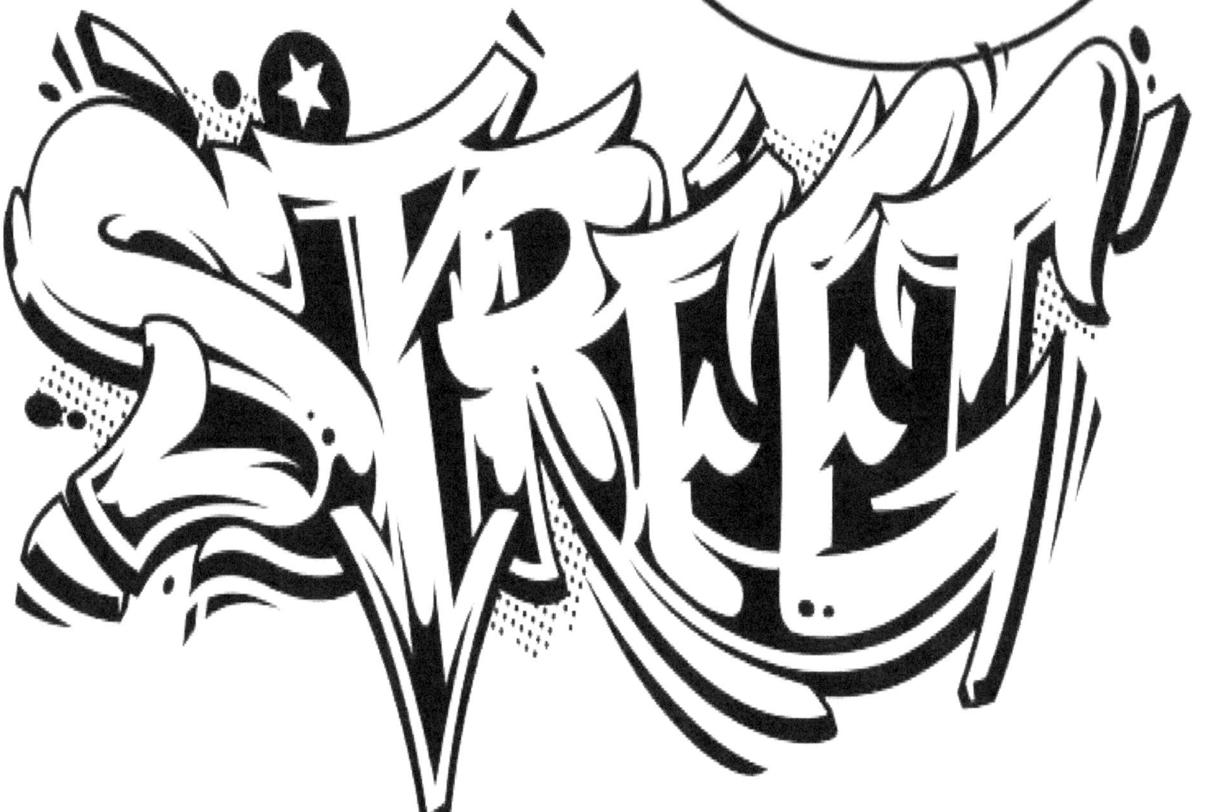

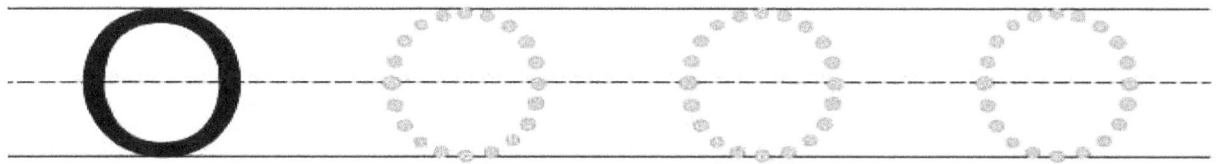

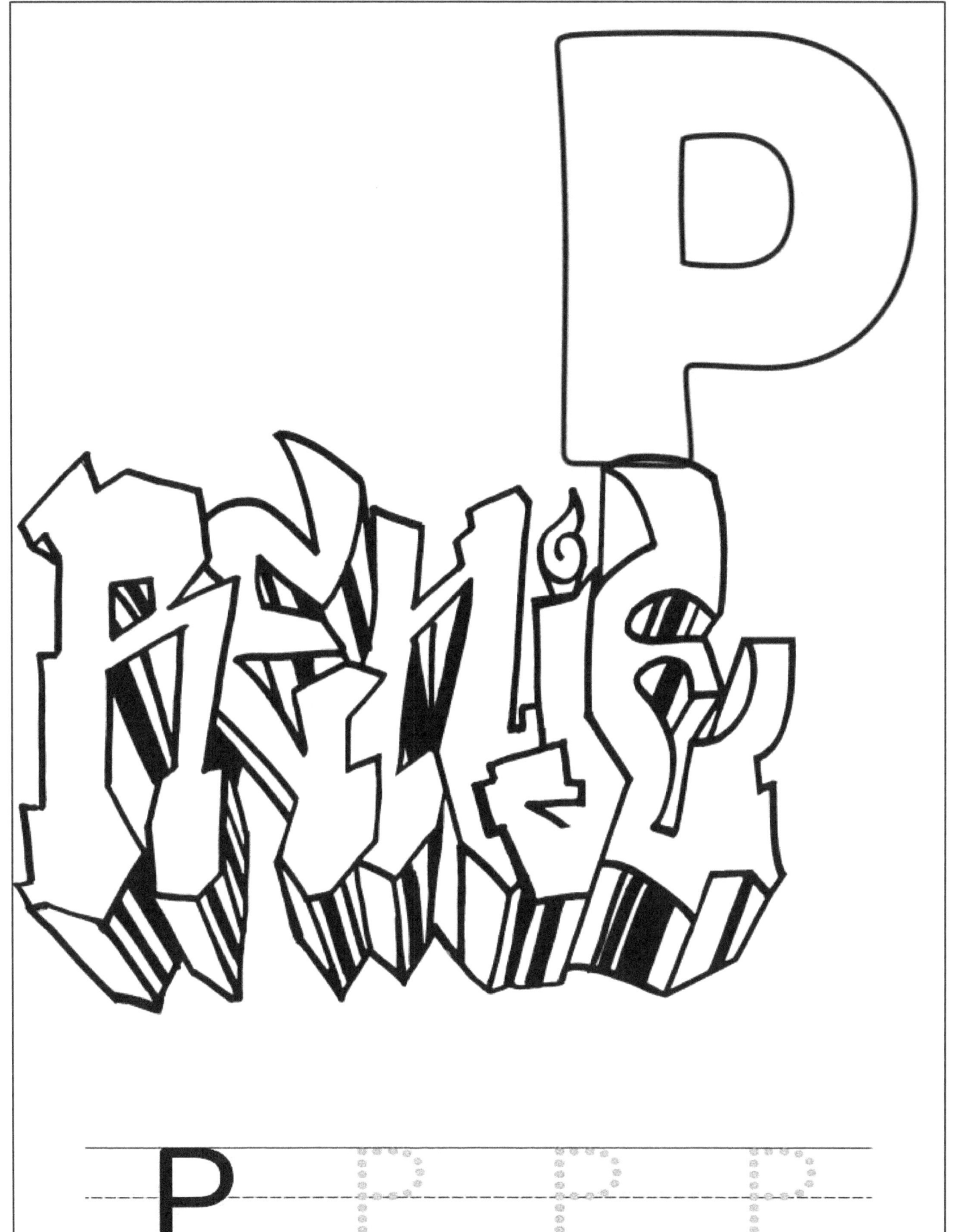

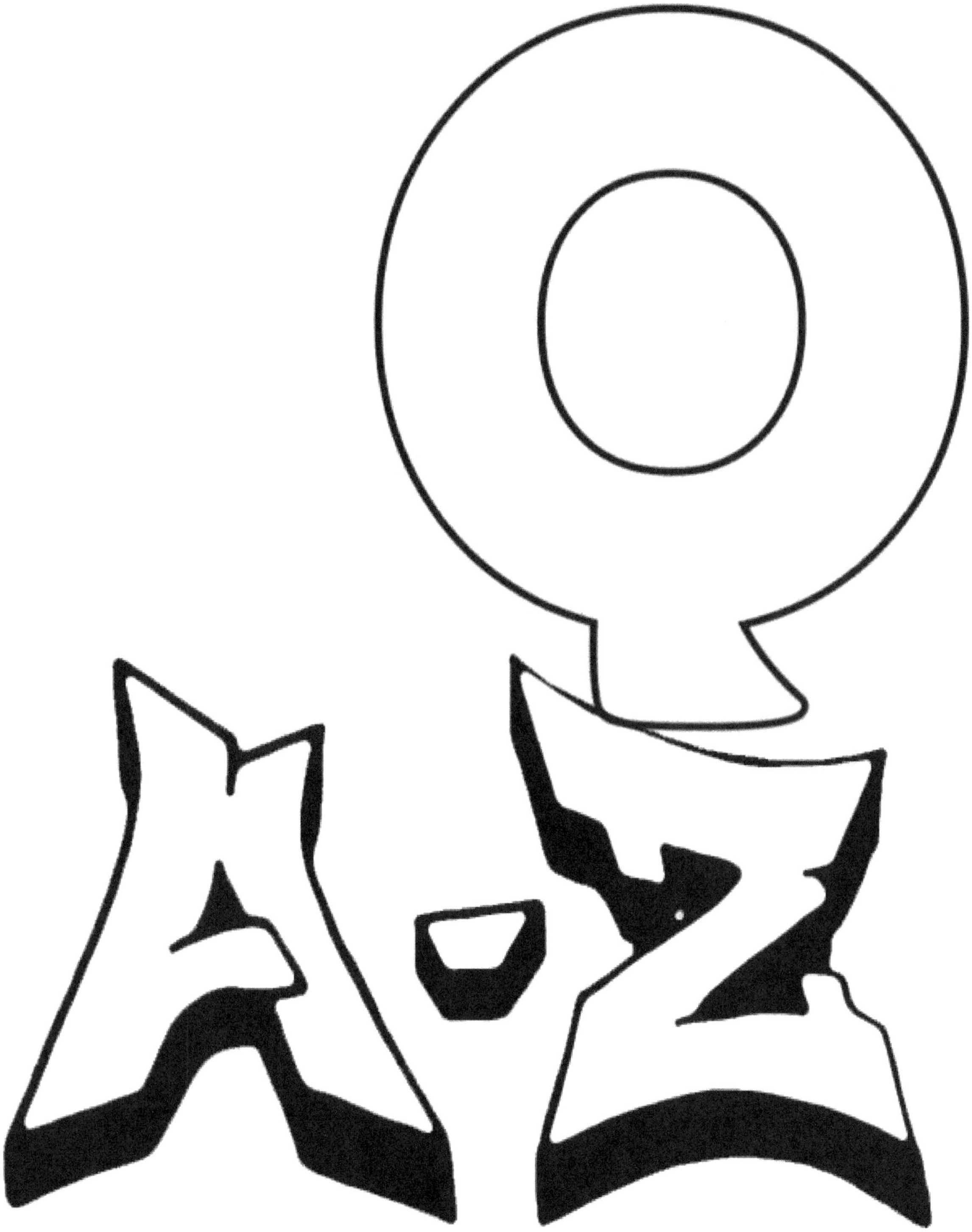

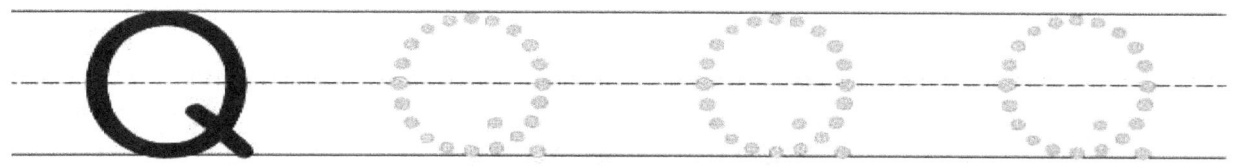

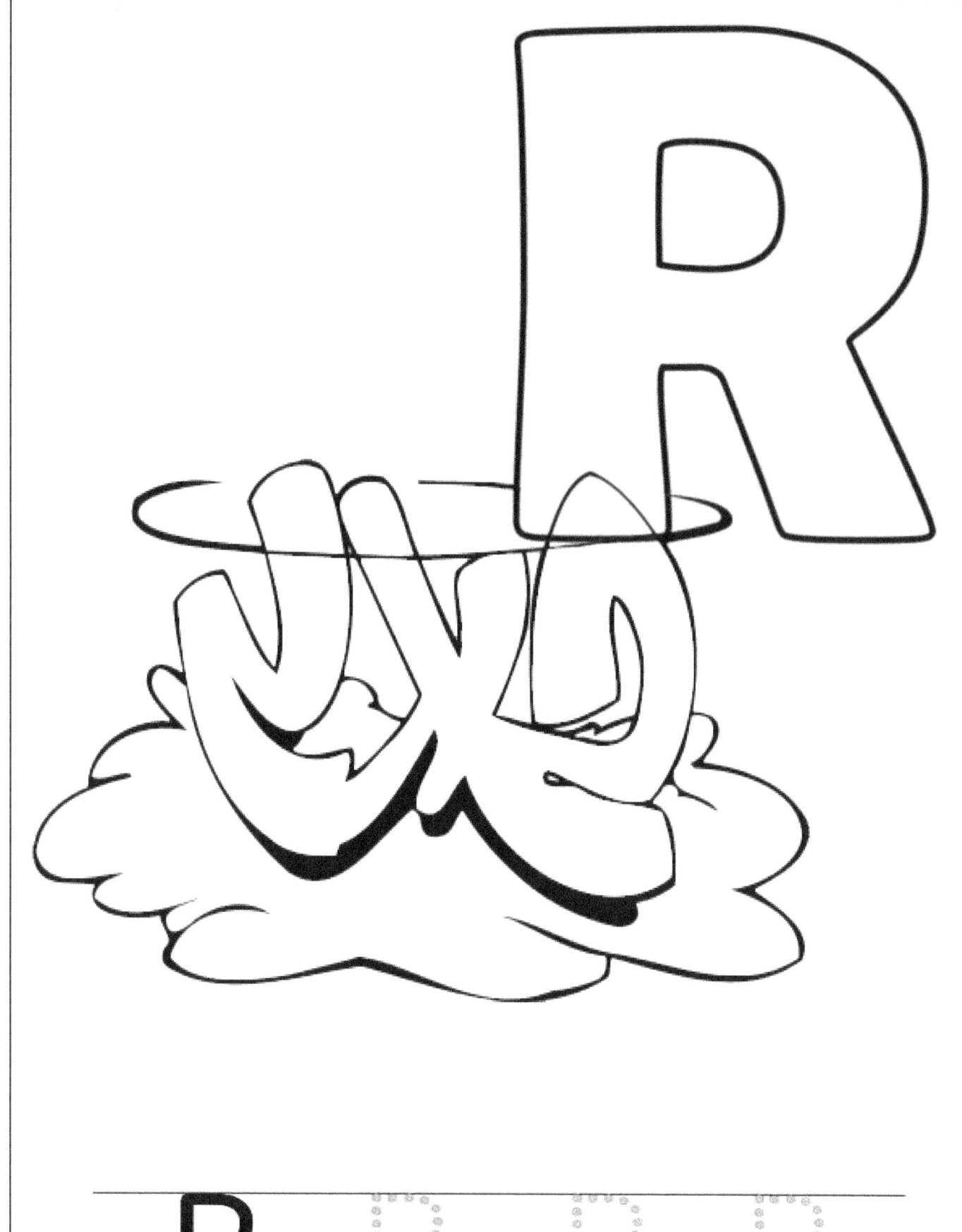

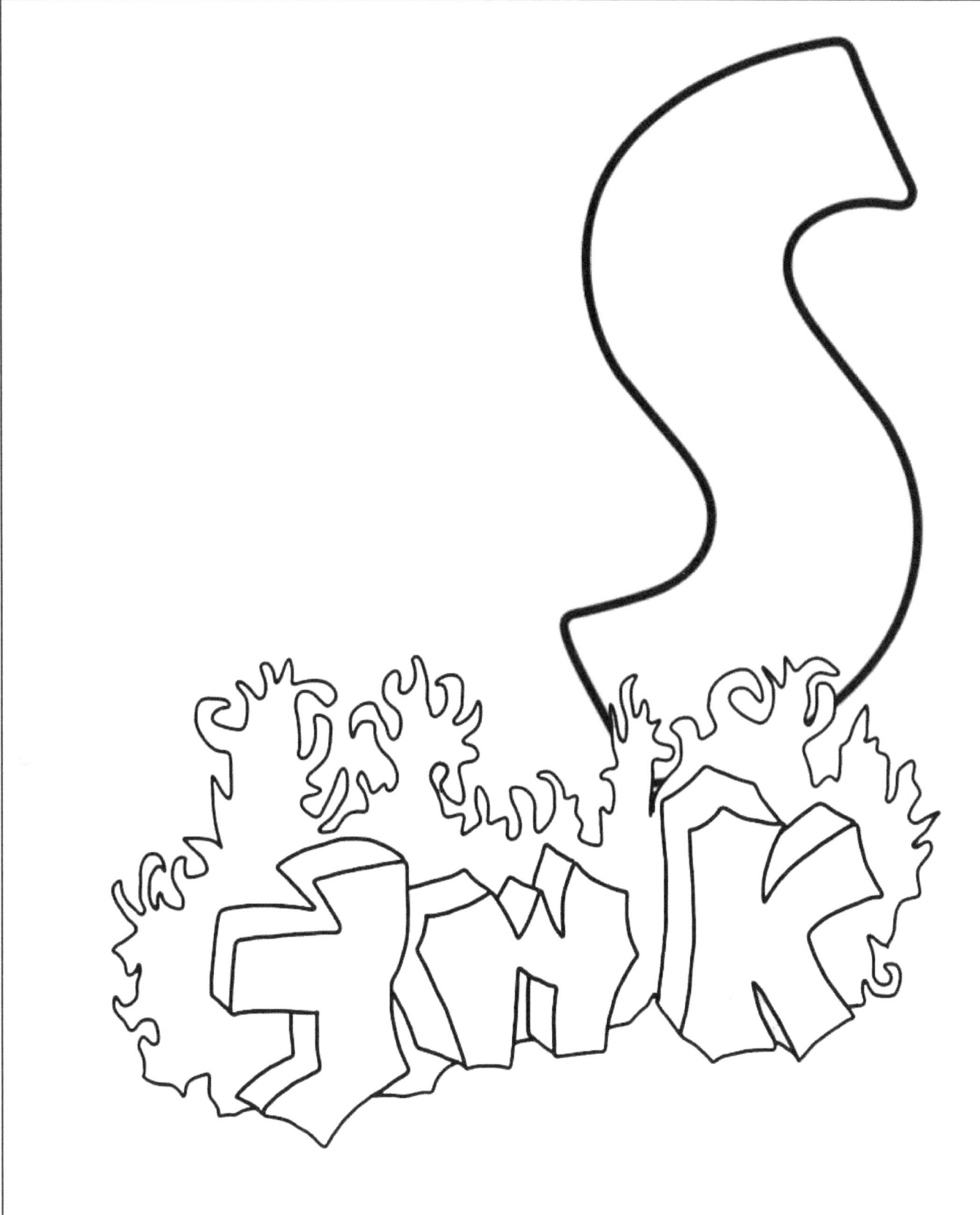

s

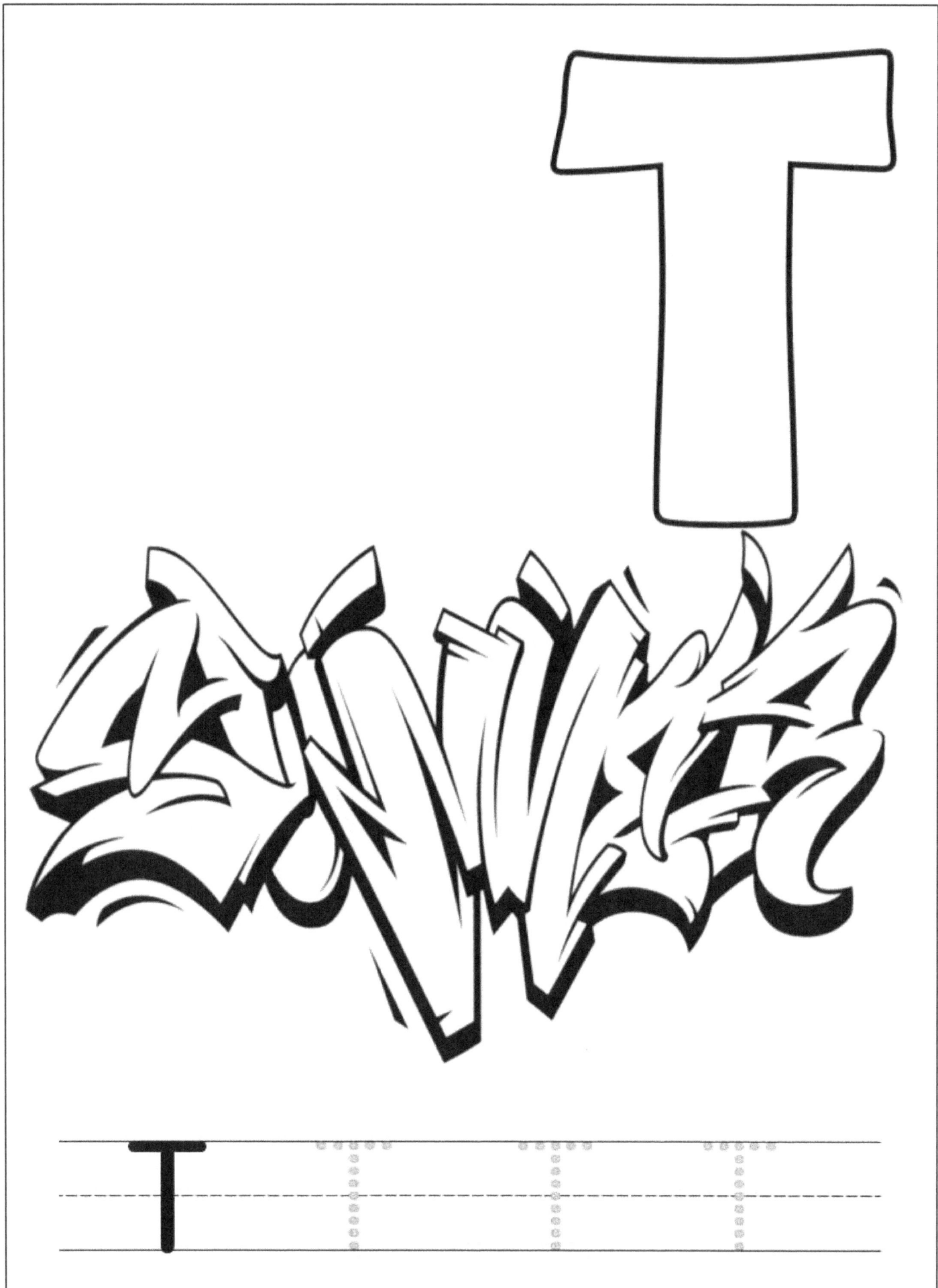

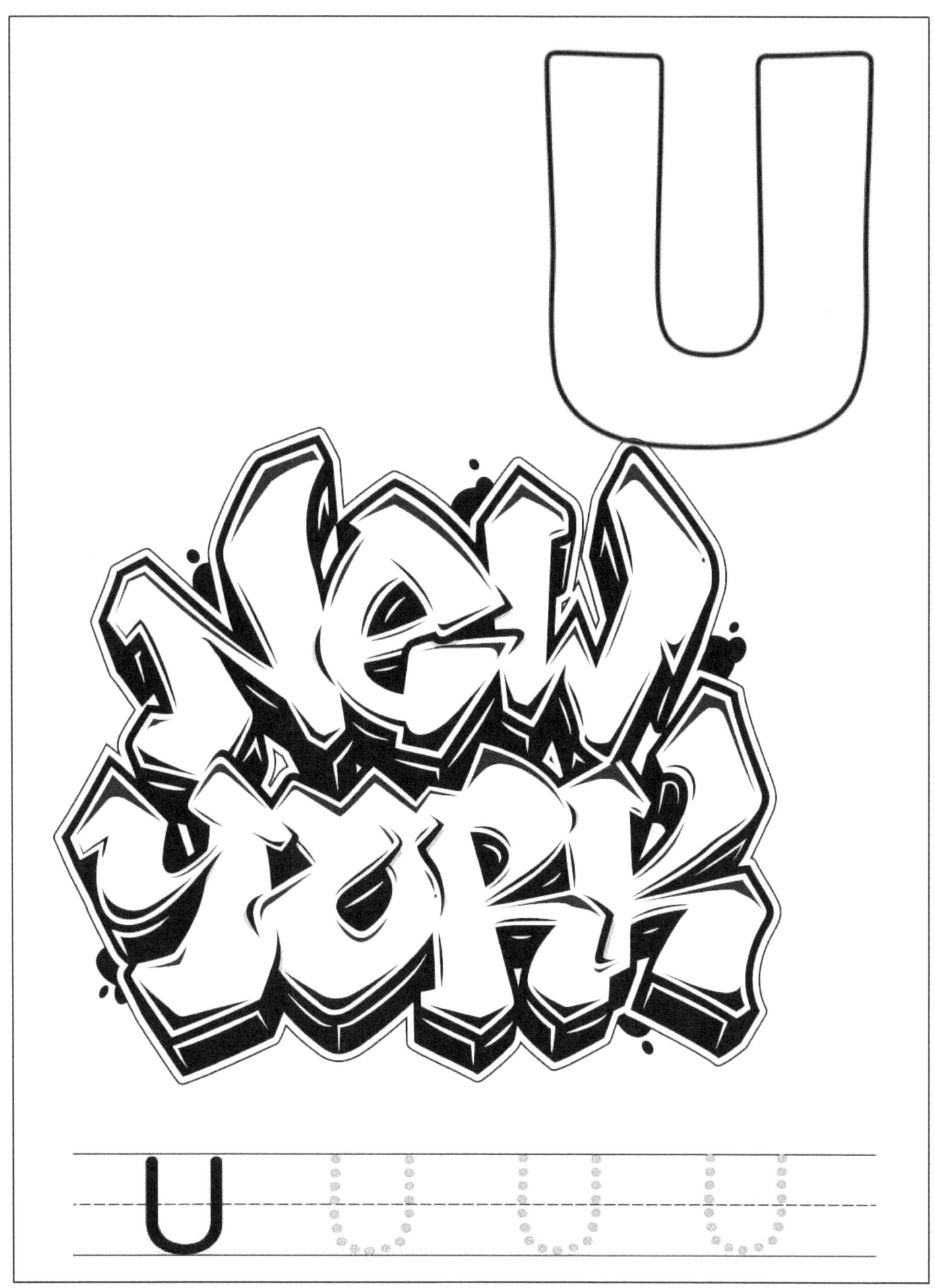

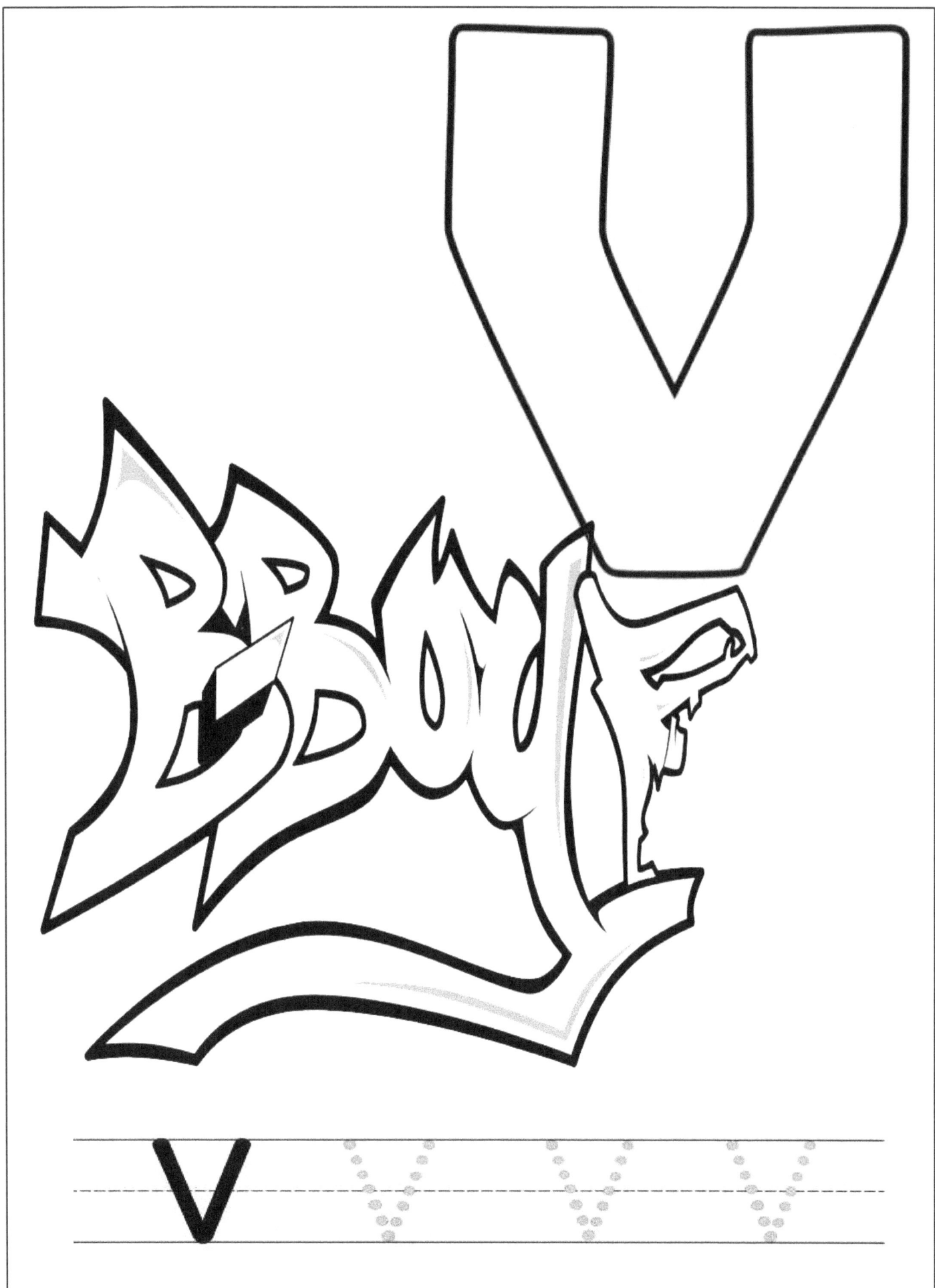

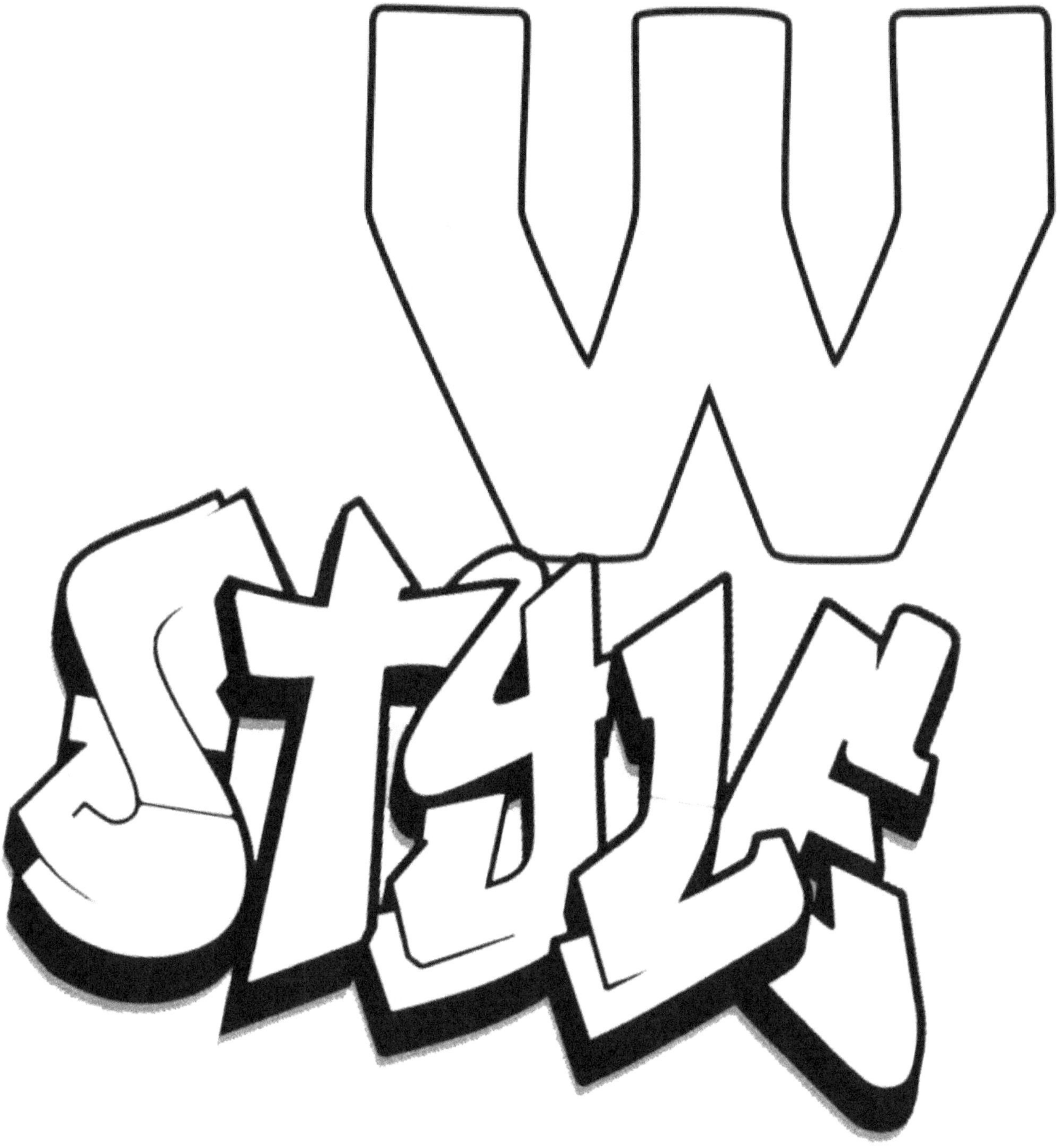

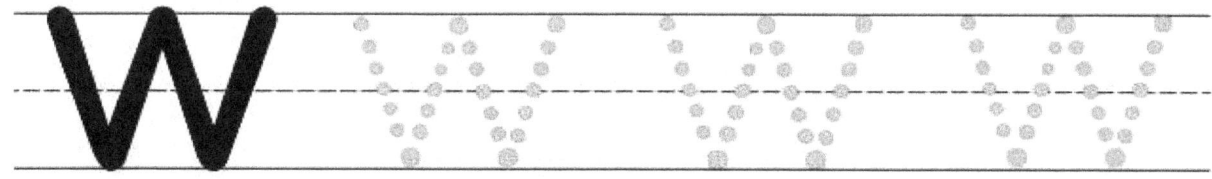

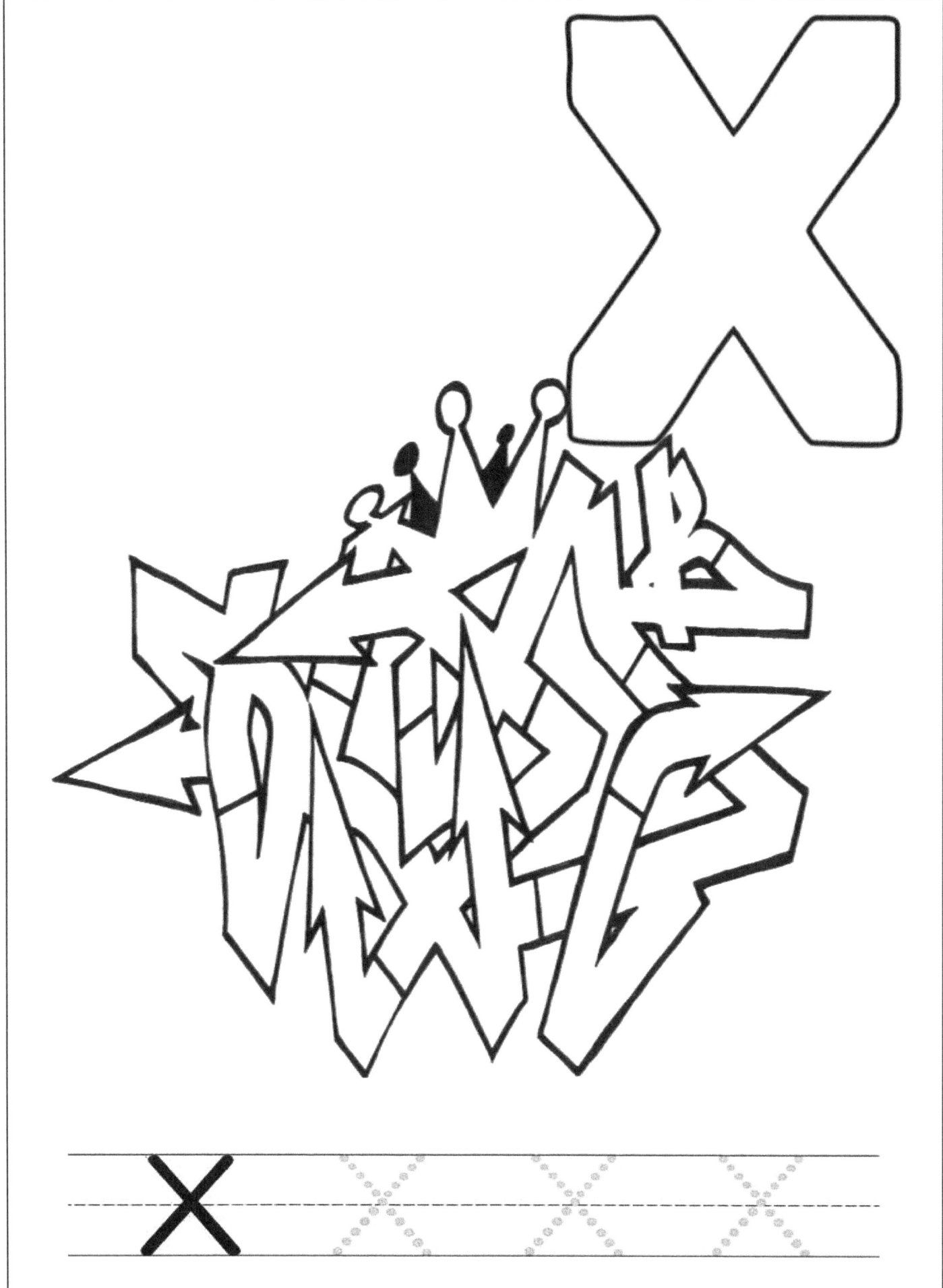

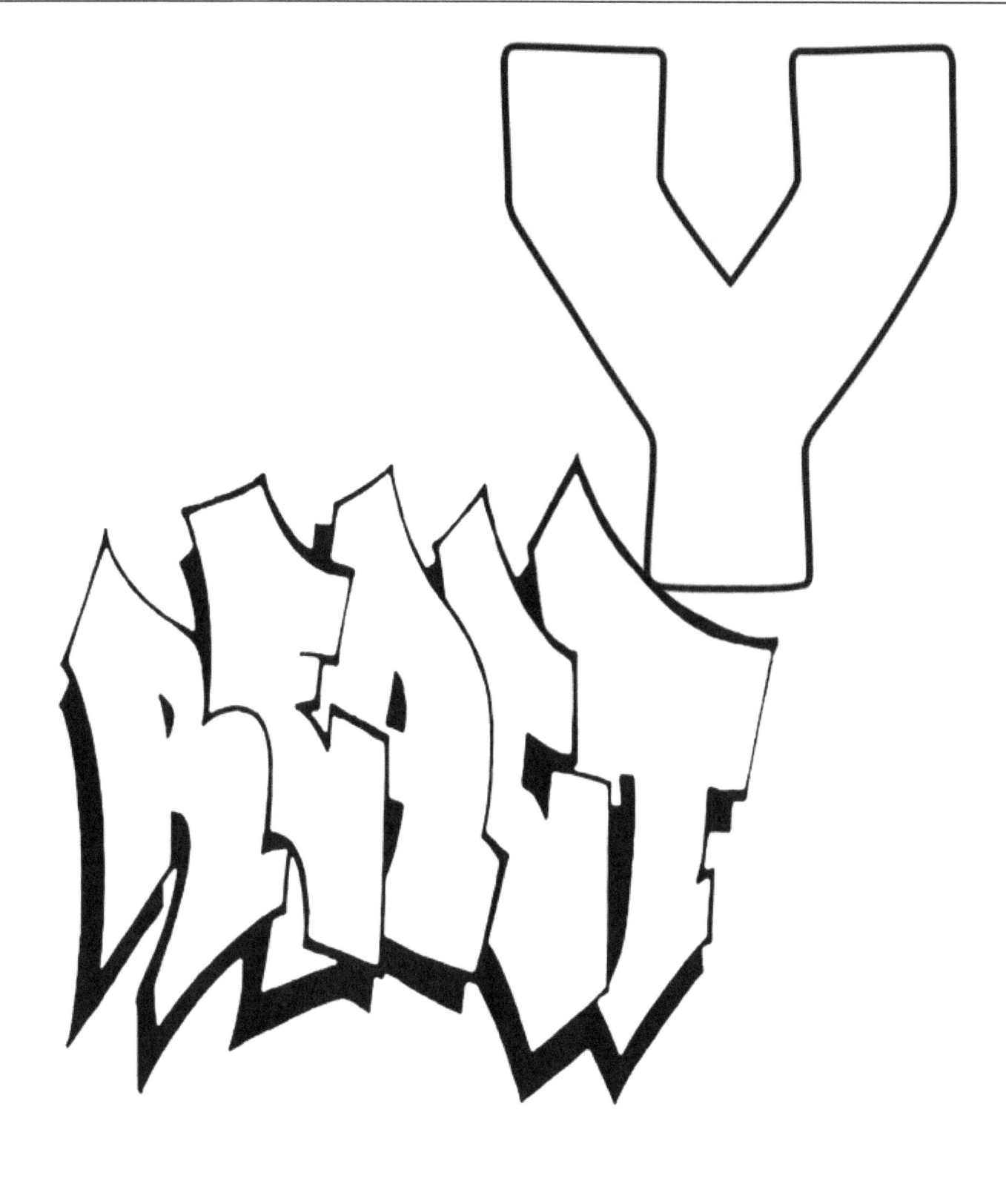

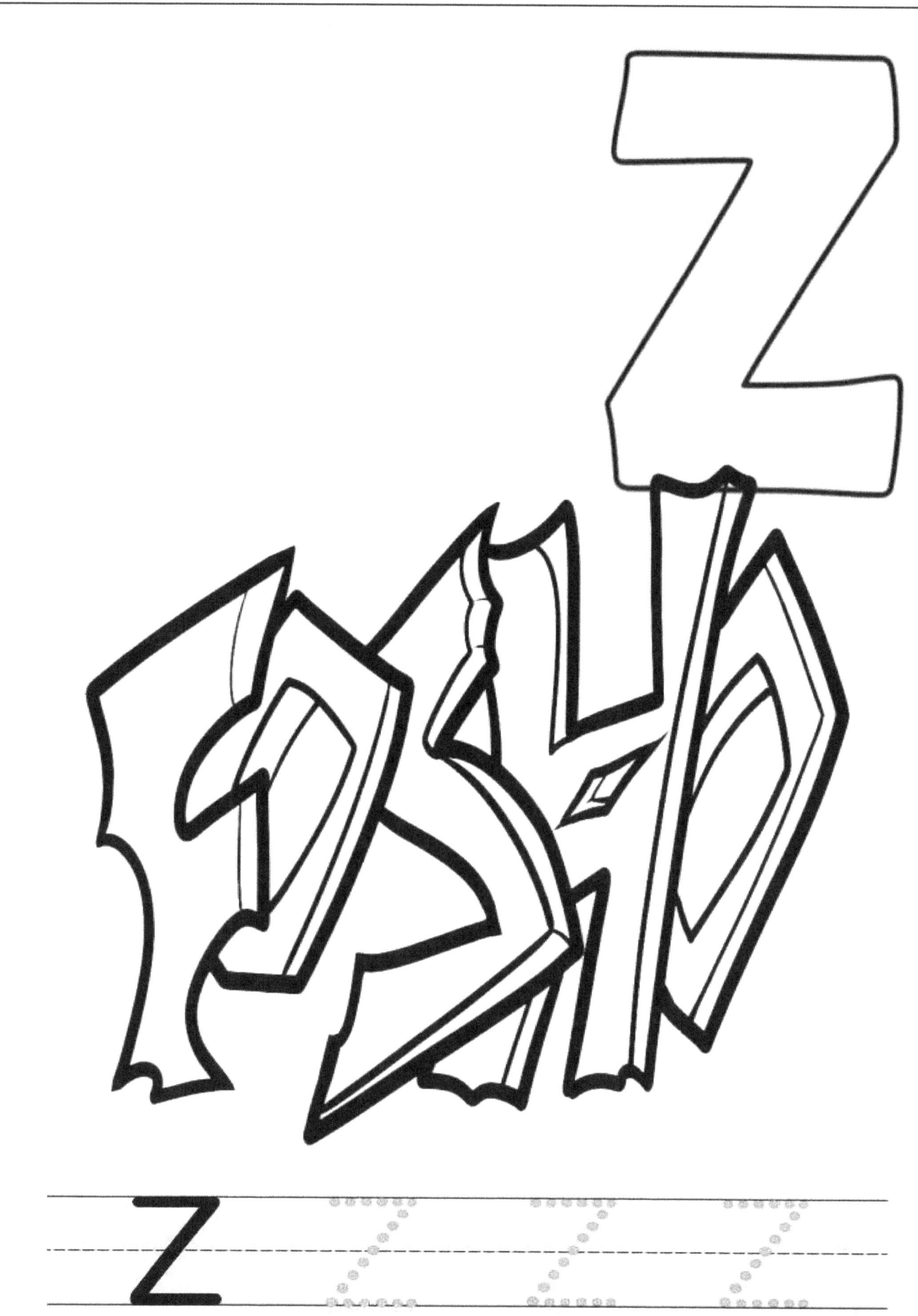

www.ingramcontent.com/pod-product-compliance
Lightning Source LLC
Chambersburg PA
CBHW081658220526
45466CB00009B/2806